Where Is Emmett Gold?

A Solve-It-Yourself Rock Music Mystery

liams and Lou Jacobs

SHOWBIZ 9/1/80

Gold Record Biggest Take-off Ever

Sound and the Fury (BSR) by Emmett Gold/Mirage recorded the best first-month sales ever for a first record by a group. Though the group has done minor work in the ...st this is its first big-time ven... ...hey leave on tour next w... ...on their s...

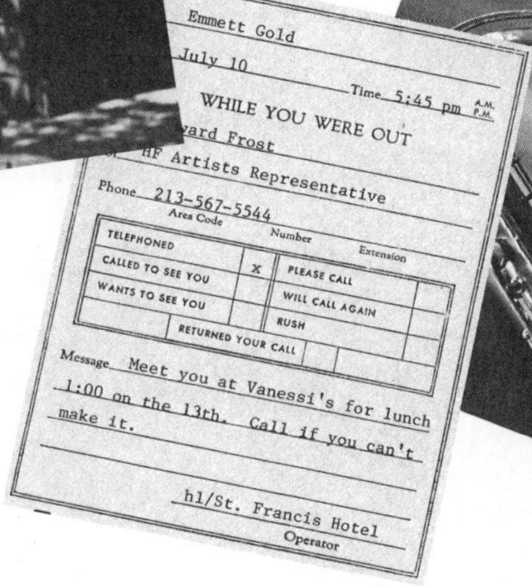

Emmett Gold

July 10

Time 5:45 pm A.M. P.M.

WHILE YOU WERE OUT

...ward Frost

...HF Artists Representative

Phone 213-567-5544

Area Code Number Extension

TELEPHONED		PLEASE CALL	
CALLED TO SEE YOU	X	WILL CALL AGAIN	
WANTS TO SEE YOU		RUSH	
RETURNED YOUR CALL			

Message Meet you at Vanessi's for lunch 1:00 on the 13th. Call if you can't make it.

hl/St. Francis Hotel

Operator

Where Is Emmett Gold?

A Solve-It-Yourself Rock Music Mystery

BY ERICA KOHL
AND HERBERT KOHL

Little, Brown and Company
Boston Toronto

FIRST EDITION

Text photographs by Erica Kohl and Nicholas King
Cover photography by Stanley Rowin
Composition by DEKR Corp., Woburn, Massachusetts
Design and production by Steam Press, Cambridge, Massachusetts

Library of Congress Cataloging in Publication Data

Kohl, Herbert R.
Where is Emmett Gold?

Summary: A rock star disappears and the reader is provided with clues to solve the mystery of his disappearance.
1. Children's stories, American. [1. Rock music—Fiction. 2. Mystery and detective stories. 3. Literary recreations] I. Kohl, Erica. II. Title.
PZ7.K8233Wh 1984 [Fic] 84-20104
ISBN: 0-316-50134-4 paperback

Published simultaneously in Canada by Little, Brown & Company (Canada) Limited

PRINTED IN THE UNITED STATES OF AMERICA

To the Reader:

Emmett Gold is missing! The rising rock star doesn't show for a major concert in San Francisco and seems to have disappeared without a trace. Is this just a temperamental musician's impulsiveness? Or something more ominous?

Donna Whitman, lawyer and private investigator, is hired to track down Gold—or at least to help explain his disappearance. As Ms. Whitman begins to pick up clues, the picture gets increasingly complicated. Are Emmett's old girlfriend and her lover somehow involved? Could one of Emmett's fans have had something to do with it? What about his family? His rivals?

You can search for answers to these questions along with Donna Whitman by examining the evidence yourself. Everything you need is included in this dossier of reports, news clippings, telephone messages, photographs, letters, plane tickets, drug prescriptions, and countless other clues. You'll need to pay close attention to details and dates. Does a phone message from the day of Emmett's disappearance have any significance? What about an old letter he wrote from Paris in 1970?

Once you've read through the evidence and reviewed it, you'll be ready to write up your own conclusions on the form provided. Then see how your own sifting, snooping, and sleuthing sizes up next to Donna Whitman's as you read her final investigative report.

Good luck!

LITTLE STAR THEATER

700 Brick Road
San Francisco, California

EMMETT GOLD
with special guest star
JOHNNY BALDW
JULY 11 &
Sat. 7:00 & 10:30 P PM: $8.75

CANCELLED

LANNA LYNN
JULY 19
Sun. 4:30 & 8:00 PM: $8.75

THE RHYTHM ROCKERS
AUGUST 7–9
Fri. 8:30 PM, Sat. 7:00 & 10:30 PM,
Sun. 8:00 PM: $9.75

Restaurant open for all shows

LITTLE STAR THEATER

HOWARD FROST
Artists' Representative

4071 Madrone Boulevard
Los Angeles, California 89701

July 12, 1981

Donna Whitman
Attorney at Law
663 Fifth Ave.
New York, NY 10026

Dear Ms. Whitman,

In the past our relationship has been limited to contract negotiations. However, I now hope that I can persuade you to work for me both as lawyer and private investigator.

You may have heard that Emmett Gold, an artist I represent, did not appear at a scheduled San Francisco concert, in which he was top billed. Gold's absence is causing me both personal and financial distress.

I don't have any confidence in the law enforcement officials that have taken on the case and believe that someone with your intimate knowledge of the music business can turn up Gold.

I really hope you will take on this case. I will be willing to take a flight to New York at your convenience to discuss the issue. Please call me collect as soon as you receive this at 213-567-5544.

Hopefully,

Howard Frost

Howard Frost

Donna Whitman
ATTORNEY AT LAW
663 Fifth Avenue, New York, NY 10026

July 16, 1981

Dear Mr. Frost,

After considering our phone call pertaining to the disappearance of Emmett Gold and researching some of the background evidence, I have decided to proceed with the investigation.

Please send any clippings, contracts, photos etc. that could illuminate Gold's past.

Sincerely,

Donna Whitman

Donna Whitman

DW/lc

Donna Whitman
ATTORNEY AT LAW
663 Fifth Avenue, New York, NY 10026

July 17, 1981

Dear Mr. Frost,

I have not received your background material on Emmett Gold as of yet. However, I have uncovered some information that might interest you. Before I go into it I want to tell you again how important it is that you provide me with an entire file on Gold, including his contracts, clippings, and any personal material that you may have access to through your own sources.

As you know, Gold's last public performance was in Portland three nights before he disappeared in San Francisco. I contacted the theater manager and he informed me that though the performance was excellent and well received, Gold had asked theater security to see that a person known in the world of music groupies as "Little Red" be kept away from backstage and at all costs out of his dressing room. Gold had also told the manager that in the past security had failed, and that this woman had been harassing him. A check with theater managers and security people in Chicago and Minneapolis showed that Gold had expressed a similar concern at previous concerts.

Have you ever heard of this person? If you have, do you know anything about her background? It seems that she might know something about Gold's disappearance, though of course it is premature to implicate her in any way.

In addition to Ms. Little Red (as I will refer to her until we have clearer identification), it seems that there has recently been some other tension within the band. I have no definite information about who has been at odds with whom, but each theater manager claimed that the band was one of the most difficult he'd had to accommodate on this year's tour circuit.

I also called journalists who reviewed the band's performances, and they informed me that Gold was brilliant onstage but seemed troubled offstage, especially when they asked him what he intended to do for his next album. Their impression was that he was not enthusiastic about being a star and kept on talking about wanting to fuse country music, electronic sound production, composition, and some kind of social or political activity. They said that they chose not to write about Gold's obsessions and in their articles (some of which are included here) concentrated on his roots, his hit record, and his current performances.

Could you fill me in on Gold's condition before the tour began? And again, please don't forget the background material.

If you would like me to continue the investigation I will want to travel to San Francisco to talk with the police there and examine any evidence Gold might have left behind. I will also want to interview the other members of the band. In order to do this I need an advance of $5,000. Please let me know immediately if you want me to go ahead.

Sincerely,

Donna Whitman

Donna Whitman

DW/lc

ROCK WORLD, JULY 16, 1981

Where did Emmett run to?

While that wild, indubitably hard rock singer, Emmett Gold, and his sizzling hot band, Mirage, were on U.S. tour, an uncanny disappearing act took place. One day before a scheduled San Francisco concert the band's tour was cancelled. No one could reach Gold and still can't. But his robust manager, Howard Frost, said, "Don't worry, all tickets will be refunded. Gold is a flexible man and the show will be back on the road before you know it."

Gold's latest album, *Lightning Strikes,* is still on the charts and it is still possible that before long Gold will turn to Platinum! In the hit single, "Lightning Strikes," a line says, "Lightning strikes but once in the same place." Let's hope that's the case here and that Gold can keep his commitments in the future.

Rumor has it that Gold and the band have not been getting along too well recently. Gold has been signed by RCA to do a solo album of old country hits, but the band isn't taking it too well.

Gold started out as a country singer and even said in a recent *Rock World* interview, "I think I'm really hittin' it big in the hard rock scene but sometimes I dream about my great ol' country band."

Has Emmett Gold gone back to Tennessee? Is he still dreaming about mountain music? Putting together a new band? Is he quitting under the pressure of fame? Can Mirage survive without their Gold? Although it's still possible that Emmett Gold and Mirage will be on stage again in no time, we're not so sure.

The world according to Tharp (and Byrne)

Is David Byrne bidding t
come the first Renai
Waver? Fresh fro
video, photography and p
projects—and tapped
duce the third B-52's
gust—the Talking
chorman is current
score for an even
choreographed
Tharp. Byrn

Grandmothers: creaky allies?

HOWARD FROST
Artists' Representative

4071 Madrone Boulevard
Los Angeles, California 89701

July 20, 1981

Dear Ms. Whitman,

I trust your legal and investigative work and would like you to continue working on finding Emmett Gold. Enclosed is the five grand you asked for. Fill me in on the results of the San Francisco investigation.

I'll try to answer the questions you raised in your letter. I've never heard of this Ms. Little Red but there certainly is some tension with groupies. Emmett has always liked his privacy and doesn't like the attention of fans and groupies. He has always preferred unlisted phone numbers and private places to stay.

Before the tour began Emmett was in great shape. With his new record taking off and with a new lucrative contract for three records in the works he was eager to get on the road. But Emmett doesn't travel very well and the tour was wearing him down. But as you know it happens to everyone on tour.

As for tension in the band, you ought to know that Emmett used to go out with our sax Liza Willow who's now living with another band member Jim Austin. Austin seems to be a fairly jealous guy and we only keep him in the band because he's a genius arranger. It's the usual band triangle which does explode every once in a while but never gets too serious.

As for my files, they're not in good condition right now. My secretary is getting them in order. Meanwhile I'll send you what's on hand. I'm enclosing some correspondence with Gold, a copy of his contract with me, some clippings on his first and second albums, and resumes of the band members.

I hope this will help you. Keep me informed on all the latest. We have to find Gold.

Yours,

Howard Frost

Howard Frost

Chicago Moon-Times, July 8, 1981

Solid Gold

This week also brings us an out-of-town event. Emmett Gold/Mirage will do two nights at Evanston. This group is mighty popular with the college set but its energy and the sophistication of its lyrics make it fine for us grown-ups, too. The band had a bit of a rocky time in Detroit, but doesn't everybody? Seems like there was a fight backstage, something about how to set up the instruments. The show was late and the band didn't get fired up until the second half. From there on in our correspondent tells us it was supersonic.

Howard Frost, the band's robust agent, tells us that it was just the matter of some rowdy roadies and assured this reporter that everything has been straightened out for the shows this week.

The single "Lightning Strikes" hit the Top 10 this week and the album *Lightning Strikes* is going strong. See you there.

THE WASHINGTON GLOBE July 9, 1981

LIMELIGHT

Emmett Gold's new album is entitled *Lightning Strikes*. Gold talked with us while pacing in his elegant suite at the Four Seasons Hotel in Georgetown. This is the fourth stop on Gold's national promotion tour for his new album.

Emmett Gold and Mirage are great on stage! The crowds and critics love 'em. It *seems* as if this hot new group will swing right up to the top, but I wouldn't bet my dollars on it. Gold and his band look, sound and *are* together on stage, but peeking backstage a minute before curtain time this "perfect" band seemed to have problems fitting together. Once on stage the puzzle pieces meshed and they played united as one. If these edgy backstage moments signify no more than the usual tour fatigue, Gold and his group will "Strike like Lightning" as they do in their hit single. If not, we'll have another flash in the pan.

HOWARD FROST
Artists' Representative

4071 Madrone Boulevard
Los Angeles, California 89701

June 15, 1980

Emmett Gold
324 West Dallas
New York, NY 10001

Dear Emmett Gold,

I have been following and watching you and your band very carefully. Yes, you have talent. But I think that I could help you do better. Just imagine: Emmett Gold/Mirage: in the BIG TIME. You'll be stars! With my help fortune is guaranteed. I'm well known coast to coast. I have an education, musical training background and plenty of experience. I know what I'm doing and I know what can help you.

You've got a nice sound and the crowds really seem to go for you, but you're missing a string somewhere. A bass guitar is what you need. And I've got a damn good one hot and ready for you. McArthur is the name. Guaranteed quality.

Take the bass and you've got me for a rep. The name may be Frost, but I'm a real fireball.

Drop me a line and I promise you won't regret it.

Yours,

Howard Frost

Howard Frost

June 21, 1980

Dear Mr. Frost,

After considerable thought I decided that we might be able to work together. I appreciate your concern for my music and acknowledge that without expert management we will have a long string of records that will disappear no matter how interesting our music was. There is only one condition I would like to make. I absolutely have to have the right to terminate our arrangement if something in me decides to go in another direction. It's not that I don't trust you. It's that I don't trust myself and need to be free to act.

Sincerely,

Emmett Gold

Exclusive Agent's Agreement Between
Howard Frost agent (4071 Madrone Blvd., Los Angeles, CA 89701) and
Emmett Gold client (324 West Dallas Street, New York, NY 10001)

Date: June 25, 1980

1) Emmett Gold agrees to have Howard Frost, artist's representative, be his sole and exclusive agent in matters pertaining to performance, reproduction, and publication of all musical and literary works composed, written, or performed, and to represent Gold in all contract negotiations and other forms of representation.

2) In exchange for these rights Howard Frost will receive a fee of 15 % of all rents and royalties of work produced or performed by Emmett Gold, and 15 % of all fees and salaries paid to Gold in his role as professional musician and composer.

3) Howard Frost agrees to provide Emmett Gold with bookkeeping and accounting services, with contract advice, and with theatrical bookings, recording dates, and publications pertaining to Emmett Gold's work.

4) Emmett Gold may terminate this contract only upon six months notice, at which time all rights to properties shall return to Gold. If such notice is not timely given, Howard Frost shall retain his share of royalties and fees for those properties placed during the term of this contract.

5) This contract shall be binding on both parties and their heirs.

Witnessed:

Julius Rosen

Julius Rosen

Signed:

Howard Frost

Howard Frost

Notarized:

Sara Swillington

Sara Swillington, CPA

Signed:

Emmett Gold

Emmett Gold

RIFFS

Glitter Gold's Game Gamble

By Katherine Stoll

Had a long day of loud music, ending at the Garden. After the screaming and the wailing I decided to slip downtown for a change of pace. Enzio's is where Juilliard meets the street, where oboe blends with sax and scat and synthesizer sound. About 2 A.M. I managed to catch Emmett Gold finishing up a set with several of Juilliard's best. I asked him what he was doing up so late the night before leaving on tour and he told me the tour was over for him, all that remained was the playing of it.

Gold's new group, Mirage, is about to make it big and yet Gold spends more time at Enzio's than in the rehearsal studio. I asked Gold about his plans for the future and got a glimpse of a complicated, serious musician that doesn't fit with the band's hard-driving image. Gold commented that he didn't want to play anymore. He went on, "Performing isn't important to me. There are major changes taking place in the sounds we can control. I see different streams of music coming together. We all have to relate to electronic music; there is no more boundary between classical music and jazz, or country and pop. Our ears are bombarded with so many sounds so finely drawn that the old scales disappear. Nobody expects classical harmony anymore just like nobody expects rhymed verse."

Gold rambled on, talking about plans to bring musicians together, about setting up small recording companies and creating new musical forms. I was half convinced but it was three-thirty and we all dream just before the morning takes us back to our boring little worlds. I should say my boring little world for Gold's world glitters. **Sound and the Fury,** his first album, is sure to go platinum and the tour should make him a celebrity. Gold's dreams of music—will they dissolve or can he make the break with success so many other musicians have dreamed of and failed to pull off? I'm not betting either way.

...stupendous world-famous ac...
special guests Gunther Gebel-Williams and Lou Jacobs.

SHOWBIZ
9/1/80

Gold Record Biggest Take-off Ever

Sound and the Fury (BSR) by Emmett Gold/Mirage recorded the best first-month sales ever for a first record by a group. Though the group has done minor work in the past this is its first big-time venture. They leave on tour next week to follow up on their success.

Band agent Howard Frost hinted that some time before the band returns it will have signed a big-money, long-term contract that will make it one of the richest groups in the industry.

London Court Case

...sibility
...tre ser-
... Ed As-
...cie Arnaz
... officially
... the Will

...nd spots has
...e country on
...the ABC and
...already con-
...how the an-
...ng to Will
...rector Mar-

...spool a two
...lation of the
...rementioned
... Circuit cur-
... of the spot
...theatres for
... spots will
... Inter-
...e an-
...een

ov...
Pe...
CBS wi...
ing in the ...
The test wi...
facilities; n...
planned at t...
said.

CBS obtaine...
ter form TDF, ...
(which has be...
tests over th...
on Mt. Sutr...
roam the B...
the over-th...

The pr...
will proba...
months...

LO...

ROCK WORLD, SEPTEMBER 14, 1980

SOUND AND THE FURY
EMMETT GOLD/MIRAGE
★★1/2

Emmett Gold/Mirage is new on the scene. The group's first album, *Sound and the Fury,* shows talent, but not much class. The music on the album is undefined. There are bits of rock and country with some atonal music thrown in. But the music and arrangements are complex, and saxophonist Liza Willow's work makes buying the album almost worthwile. Gold and drummer Rob Bangor are from Tennessee, Willow is from the Berklee College of Music, pianist Jim Austin is a Juilliard graduate, and bass guitarist J. D. McArthur comes out of hard rock. These musicians display an impressive array of talent and each of them shows off virtuoso skills on one number or another. If they can ever bring this combination together, we may be in for some interesting music. Until then, they can sure use some practice time. Let's hope that this first album does not provide a one-way trip home for all musicians involved.

ROCK WORLD, JULY 2, 1981

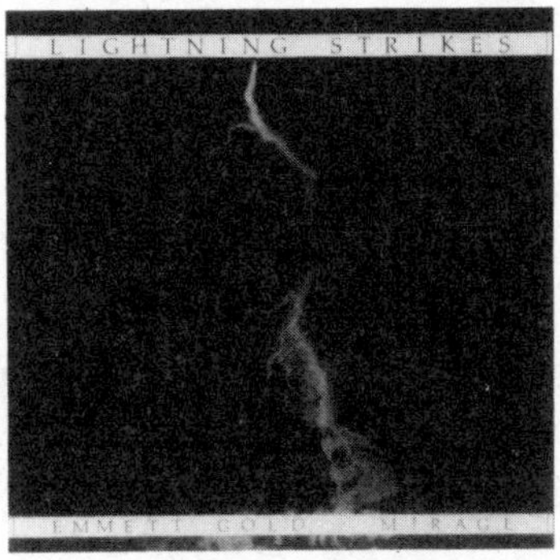

LIGHTNING STRIKES
EMMETT GOLD/MIRAGE
★★★★

A group of diverse, brilliant musicians has found a way to organize its unique skills and put it all together in a fiery, showy, driving album that should set new standards for contemporary musicians. Imagine putting Juilliard together with country music, hard rock with the sophisticated jazz of the Berklee School of Music, and coming out with one fabulous sound. That's what Emmett Gold/Mirage has pulled off and you have to hear it.

This group of extraordinary musicians has no single leader. Emmett Gold, the composer, lead singer, and guitarist, is matched by the sensational Liza Willow, who plays a funk saxophone with Coltrane and Charlie Parker thrown in—the Berklee influence in the band. Pianist Jim Austin's arrangements keep everything tight, and just when it seems that one musician or another might throw off the balance, the ensemble comes together and takes us back to the song itself. Rob Bangor, the drummer, keeps a steady heavy beat that is reinforced by the brilliant electric bass of J. D. McArthur. The album has some slow laments and love songs and a number of driving songs. It's for crying, dancing, and mostly listening—our choice for best of the year so far.

Resume

Elizabeth O'Neill
Stage Name: Liza Willow
432A West End Ave.
New York, NY 10027

Born: February 16, 1952
Bear Cave, Michigan

Music Education

- Interlocken Music Camp, Interlocken, Michigan. 1966-1968
  Specialized in saxophone; second instrument--piano
- Berklee College of Music, Boston, Massachusetts. B.A. 1977

Scholarships and Awards

- Beecham Scholarship to study at the Nadia Boulanger School in Paris. Summers 1970-1971
- Second Prize, Saxophone Competition at the Pinewood Music Festival, Los Angeles, California. December 1975
- Composition Prize for "Sonata #1: Daybreak," Hyman Music Foundation, Boston, Massachusetts. 1976

Relevant Work Experience

- Interlocken Music Camp Instructor. Summers 1973-1974
  Taught saxophone and music theory
- Studio Musician, EML Studios, London. 1972-1973
  (saxophone, keyboard, vocals)

Record Credits

- Modern Classical Music, London Symphony Orchestra (EML Records, London, 1977)
- Courthouse Jazz, The Jazz Quintet (RV Records, Amsterdam, 1970)
- Between the Lines, The Fragments (KPS Records, Liverpool, 1977)
- Dictation, Rod Bentley's Blues Band (Fly Me Records, London, 1978)
- Sound and the Fury, Emmett Gold/Mirage (Back Street Records, New York, 1980)
- Lightning Strikes, Emmett Gold/Mirage (Back Street Records, New York, 1981)

Perfomance Credits

- Stoneyridge Jazz Festival, Stoneyridge, Massachusetts. Fall 1973, 1974
- Club musician with the following groups: The Hayfever Jazz; Rex; The Jazz Quintet; The Fragments; Rod Bentley's Blues Band. 1973-1978
- Emmett Gold/Mirage. 1980-present

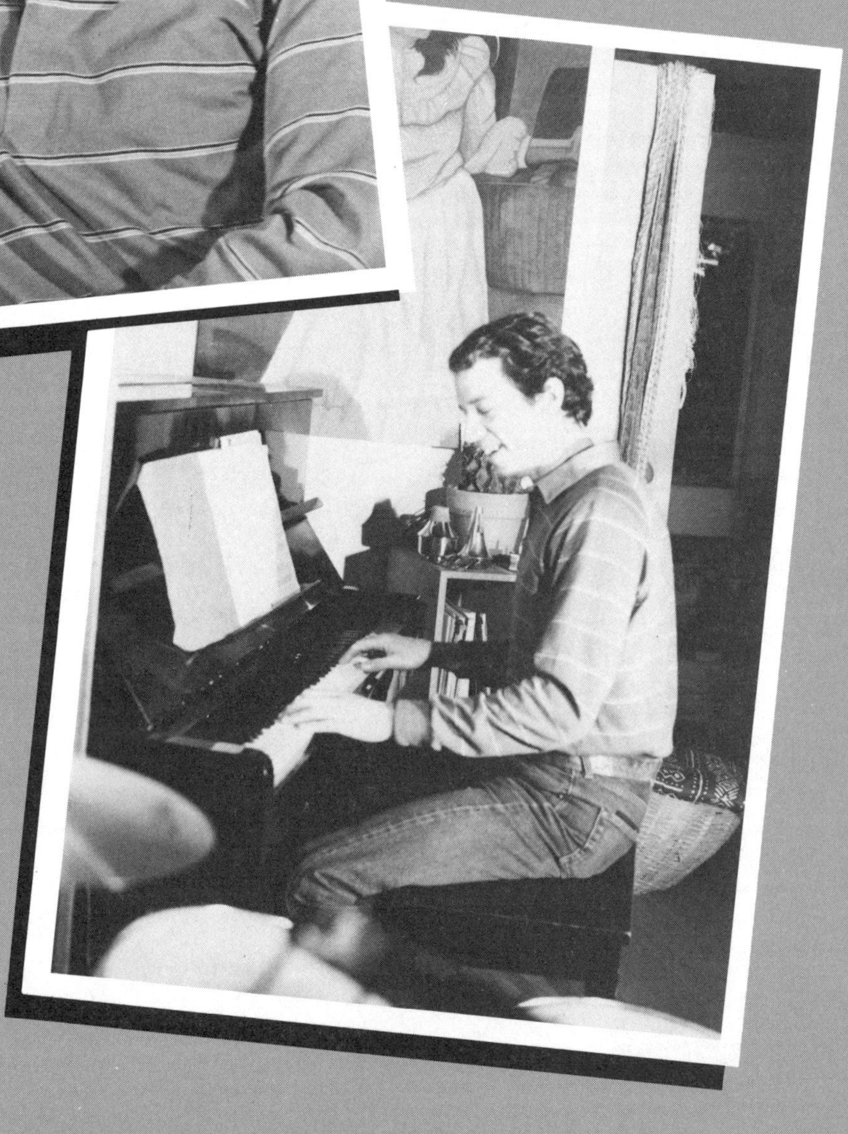

Resume:

Jim Austin
432A West End Ave.
New York, NY 10027

b. Sept. 9, 1952
Cleveland, Ohio

Piano student Frank Loesser 1962-1972

Occasional rehearsal pianist
Cleveland Philharmonic Symphony (until graduated Juilliard)

Juilliard School of Music, B.A. 1976
Major: piano and composition

Marlboro Summer Festival, 1972-1976
Student master classes

Sound Assistant, Newport Jazz Festival

Awards: Second Prize, Stein Composition Award for piano trio with synthesizer, 1977

Honorable Mention, Field Competition for Voice Composition for Variations on a Theme by Billie Holiday, soprano with piano accompaniment, 1979

First Prize, Vienna Electronic Composition Competition for Fugue and Fugative Synthetic Piano #1, 1980

Performance Experience

Performing Member: Undergraduate piano Quintet, modern jazz ensemble, Julliard, 1972-1976
Columbia Jazz Ensemble, 1976-1977
New York Chamber Orchestra, 1978
Free Form Synthesis, 1979
The Alice Fine Experience, 1976-1979
Emmett Gold/Mirage, 1980-present

Record Credits

Sound and the Fury - Emmett Gold/Mirage (Back Street Records, NY 1980)
Lightning Strikes - Emmett Gold/Mirage (Back Street Records, NY 1981)

Resume

John David McArthur
Stage Name: General J. D. McArthur
127 East 12th St.
New York, NY 10025

Born:
July 10, 1947
Cincinnati, OH

Musical Background

- Learned acoustic guitar and electric bass from Rick Steel of the Cincinnati Heads
- Backup bass for the Cincinnati Heads 1963-66
- Studied electric guitar with Smith James in Chicago 1966-67
- Music major at City College of Chicago 1971-73

Performance Credits and Professional Experience

- Bass guitar in club dates with Cincinnati Heads, Rockets, Deep Five, Bill Barton and Friends 1964-67
- USO performances in Southeast Asia 1968-70
- Studio Soundmixer, HF Sound Inc. 1974-76
- Sound Technician and stand-in bars for Caravan Associates 1975-77
- Electric bass with Grand Avenue 1977-78
- Hard Knocks, Composer and Arranger 1979-80
- Mirage, Composer and Arranger 1980-present

Record Credits

- Sound and the Fury - Mirage (Back Street Records, NY 1980)
- Lightning Strikes - Mirage (Back Street Records, NY 1981)

Resume: Rob Bangor

Rob Bangor (born Robert Barker, July 10, 1952, Mt. View Hollow, Tennessee)

Instruments:

drums and all forms of percussion from washboard bass to cow bells and congo drums.

Band Experience:

Mutt and Jeffrey
Country Heaven
The Cincinnati Boys
One Night Stand
Philadelphia Dreaming
The East Coast Ramblers
Emmett Gold/Mirage

Drummer on numerous records produced by:

Mountain Discs
Cincinnati Records
Blue Top Inc.

Recordings:

Sound and the Fury
Emmett Gold/Mirage
Back Street Records

Lightning Strikes
Emmett Gold/Mirage
Back Street Records

EMMETT GOLD:

b. Dec. 30, 1952
Mt. View Hollow, Tennessee

Musical Experience:
Mutt and Jeffrey 1967-68
Cliff and the C-Minors 1968-69
Emmett Gold/Mirage 1980-present

Apprentice: Composition Performer
Barney Robertson, Paris 1970-72
Studio work, Europe 1970-72
(backup guitar and vocals)

Performed in New York at:
Hitching Post 1972-75
Cafe 7 1975-76
Amdeck 1975-79
Hagar's 1978-80

Compositions:
Down and Out
Regal St.
Up from Tennessee
Back Again
Hardest of Times
Wistful Thinking
Masquerade
Blue Flame
Roads to Freedom (Paths to Hell)
Make a Switch
Orders to Go
Lightning Strikes
Black Arrow
Blood to Shed
A Tangled Mind
Captain Red

Recordings: <u>Sound and the Fury</u>
Emmett Gold/Mirage
(Back Street Records NY, 1980)
<u>Lightning Strikes</u>
Emmett Gold/Mirage
(Back Street Records NY, 1981)

July 19

Dear Ms. Donna Whitman,

I recently heard from Howard and a few other various sources that you are the investigator researching the disappe rance of Emmett Gold. I am xerk gdes very closely aquainted to Emmett. Besides being his drummer I've grown up with Emmet Gold and through the years we have aquired a valuable friendship. I Hhear and believe that you are a very reliable investigator, care about your cases and do a very thorough job. This is one case that I think I can hxlpc you on. I know Emmetts ways and habbits and am worried of what may become of him. If I can't help you, I don't know who can.

The most recent condition Emmett was in is a familiar one to me/. Growing up and going to school with Emmett I've grown to be used to his moods and whaßß what they mean. Show biz has put pressure on him. Many of his childhood expressions are being found on his face lately, I've noticed.

xnstcw When Emmett and I first began to play together we were just "Freshman nothings". When we hit the school big with "Mutt & Jeffery" alot of hhe kids began to xxxss accept us, everyom but rival musicians. Many times other small bands who used to be the "high school hit" played with us. But we, more and more frequently, becam e the major part of gigs and concerts.

Our backups (who used to be stars) began to threaten us for taking their place. This was just pure childish jealousy but it was the bkg one thing that seemed to bother Emmett. He would act edgy and never seem quite comfortable. Recently he has been acting in that same way.

I'm not blaming anyone or accusing anyone of harassing Emmett but I do know Emmett inside and out and someone, somewhere, somehow isx bothering him. Lately there has been friction within the band and I think Emmetts position as a star may be at stake. I can't single anyone out but I tt think Emmett is escaping the torture of someone's pressure.

I know Emmett and I know when he needs help. And I believe me he needs it now. I think thats what he's looking for. You probably need all of the information you can get and knowing that I care about this person more than anyone I'll give you what I've got.

I went through school with Emmett and enclosed xxx are many high school memories, letters and things about Emmett you may need to know.

Lets wish for good luck!

Sincrely,

Rob Bangor

June 6, 1968

FAREWELL SENIORS!

Dear Seniors,

As the year draws to a close and you near the end of your high school career, I find that I am filled with pride and sadness.

The staff and I feel so pleased that you have accomplished this goal and are moving on to the world of higher learning, or the world of work. You, also, must feel a sense of accomplishment after four years of working so hard. We know that you will be successful persons at whatever you decide to do.

We are sad because we will miss you, and after four years you have become like family. But we know that this is just the beginning for you and we are excited for you. Good luck to all of you!

John Harding

THE HIGH SCHOOL HIT!

We would like to share a little of the hidden talent here at Macumber High. I bet you don't know that Emmett Gold and Robert Barker, the ones that are seen locally hanging out with the gang at the soda shop, are actually the sensational high-school band Mutt and Jeffrey themselves. Well, yesterday the Macumber Viewer caught them off stage and decided to have a chat. Here's what we've learned:

V: How did Mutt and Jeffrey get started?

G: We first got together in seventh grade.

B: We were kind of different. Knowing his tallness and my shortness we really didn't fit in with the other guys.

G: Since we both had an interest in music we decided to get together. I've always been interested in music because of my folks and I guess Barker was just born to rhythm.

B: Since I was always an outcast it brought me even closer to my born talent.

V: When did you first play in public?

G: My mom and dad were having a big 25th anniversary party and most of the band didn't show so my Uncle Roscoe asked us to do everybody a favor and help out the band.

B: Yeah, that really gave us our starting confidence. People must have liked us because from then on we've had requests coming out all over the place.

V: What do you intend to do with your music in the future?

B: Well, I plan to work my way through junior college playing lots of gigs.

G: I really want to get serious with music so I plan to take a break from playing and start studying. Some day I hope to be like Bob Dylan who writes songs and arranges music along with playing and singing.

V: Well, it looks like Mutt and Jeffrey have a good future ahead of them. And I hope we see all you readers at the upcoming Sweethearts Ball which will be featuring Mutt and Jeffrey.

SENIORS

KIM BAKER who
uary, is attending
terinarian Receptio
cisco and is curren
Lewis in Gualala.
SABRINA BROWN
from the Netherlan
diploma and will
Santa Cruz where s
majoring in psyc
guages.
KRISTEN CHRIST
exchange student
wants to go to col
Equestrian Scienc
liked her Indepen
Equestrian Scienc
HERMAN COLE
field College in
gon. After gradua
to be a History t
coach. He liked
shop best at MH
SEAN GREEN
Air Force as a
cialist, and whe
he'd like to maj
ence. He liked
vacations most
BRENDA JON
modeling and
tion College in
she liked most
friends.
DESIRAE M
work followin
her senior y
most at MHS.
TODD PHILL
sen County
Ca. and stu
The thi
footb
PA
Ro
on
p

SWEET

BALL

WHEN: FEBRUARY 14Th VALENTINES DAY

WHERE: MACUMBER HIGH GYM

featuring **LIVE**

our own fabulous

MUTT and JEFFREY

CANCELLED

$1.00 —a person

$1.50 a couple

Knoxville Ledger Oct. 15, 1969

...costu...
...music by the Miriam Dvo...
Orchestra.

Tickets cost $10 at the door, or $9 at United Savings, the Village Shop and KTOB Radio. For information, phone

...oma Co...
Dance, the Tahitian ...
singer Miriam Dvorin. The Unio...
tural Hispana will present dances from Panama, Columbia and Ecuador, and

Music Notes

Cliff and the C-Minors Become Major

Cliff and the C-Minors were a major hit at the County Fair last week. Their musical float won first prize in the Country Time Parade. Each member, Cliff Livingston, Bob Hagar, Sue Randlin, Jaramy Winston, Harlow Ringer, and Emmett Gold received blue ribbons and a few six pax to celebrate the occasion with. The group owed its prize to the enormous cowboy hat that was mounted as a canopy over the large flatbed truck as the group plucked out old country tunes under the shade of the brim on a 90° Cranson Honer Day. I'm sure everyone who saw the fascinating float was convinced to drop by Malcomb's Tap next Friday and tune in on Cliff and the C-Minors during their opening night appearance.

he's ...

By ROBIN...
Copley News...
HOLLYWOO...
ades ago Stevie W...
little 10-year-old wit...
in himself.

Could he sing, h...
member of the ...
group.

Replied Stevie: ...
better than Smoke...

And events sh...
Even Smokey ...
agrees with that a...

Generally rate...
creative geniuses...
list of hits seems...

January 15, 1970

To ALL MY FRIENDS and FAMILY

I'm leaving Tennessee! Maybe not forever but I just got to get out. Got an opportunity to learn about different music. And there's no way that I'm gonna turn down that at this time in my life. This is no sudden decision. I've been thinking about it for quite a while. RIXX Playing music is great but I can't really express myself playing other people's stuff. I need to travel, I need to grow and I need to learn. I don't want any of you to back out on what you've gotta do. That goes for me too. So I gotta start now and someday I'll be singing my own music. Paris is where I'm needed. Don't try to get ahold of me I wanna be on my own. Don't worry either cause I'll keep in touch.

Emmett

P.S. Please share this note with all who are concerned.

Mutt,

I had to write a little extra on yours. I'm gonna miss ya— jamming together working together. It's just that I need a while on my own. I promise to keep in touch and I know we'll play together again— maybe even some of my music.

don't you give up,

Jeff

TO Robert Barker BACK HOME

Dear Mutt, March 10, 1970

I don't know if I'm still Jeffrey. at 5 every afternoon when we used to practice I miss you and our music but the rest of the time — it's too new to think of anything else but being here. My eyes and ears are opening but my pocket is having troubles. I need money but somehow don't care.

I live in a box, no shower or hot water but it's not much different than the cabins at home except that there's all kinds of people like me running from something and grabbing on to new things. Write me at American Express, Rue de l'Opera Paris and keep banging away. Emmett

TO: Rob Barker
Field Hotel Grey St.
Chicago, Ill 46012

May 12, 1972

Mutt —

Paris and Europe are over — it's time to step out again, to get back on stage. I've got some wonderful song ideas and need you and your rhythms. How about coming to New York?

Mom told me you were in Chicago and have been touring alot. I don't have anything much to offer but a couch and some food and music to share, but I know we can make it. Had a dream last night of us playing together again. If you would like to join me I can scare up a one way Greyhound ticket from Chicago and I'll even meet you at the bus stations.

Hopefully,

~~Emmett~~ Jeff

(my address — 324 W. Dallas
NY 10001)

HOWARD FROST
Artists' Representative

4071 Madrone Boulevard
Los Angeles, California 89701

July 21, 1981

Dear Donna,

I feel that it is important to communicate with you about my personal feeling about Gold. I am worried that his disappearance is more serious than I imagined because whatever complaints he has ever made he always shows up--sometimes at the last second but he's there when the group has to perform. I've been thinking and worrying about him since we talked and have some major suspicions. I see Emmett as a very weak person. He runs from place to place and from musical idea to musical idea. He also lets himself get overwhelmed by things that intimidate him. For example he's never been able to accept the fact that Jim Austin and Liza Willow have the kind of musical training that makes it easier for them to deal with changes of style and fashion than he can.

Gold is a very bitter person. He would have been better off if he grew up in a city and went to a good school instead of being a self-taught country boy.

Austin's technical training as well as Willow's amazing technique have been a problem for him from the moment the band was formed. What has been bothering me is Gold's foolish dreams about being Beethoven or Mozart. He's got this idea of escaping to be a genius which sometimes becomes manic and suicidal. He just can't accept who he is and sometimes I see him hating himself. He fights to get hurt and I've seen him hurt himself. That's why I'm so worried. He has these foolish fantasies about being a serious musician just when he's about to be a success. That success is what I see him running away from. He's good and I care about him but he's hard to reach.

Maybe this rambling letter won't be of much help but I had to tell you about my feelings for Gold and my concern for his ability to take care of himself.

Sincerely,

Howard

P.S.: Enclosed is a correspondence between Gold and McArthur, one of the band members, that I dug out of my files. It may interest you.

July 26, 1980

Dear M,

looks like were going to do it. Talked to Frost a nd he cried for joy jumped and shouted-- theres new music in sight............

its you and me boy YOU AND ME I can see it now!!!

McArthur lands gold

The One and Only country-Military-Rock and roll-Star-filled-musical experience. Theres no way we can't be good, be Gold, be Platinum!!!

This is it for now but not for long

The General with the pick

July 28, 1980

Dear JD,

I read your letter with interest. There seems to be a misunderstanding. I would be delighted to work WITH you but did not have such a close collaboration in mind. At this point I have quite a number of other musicians — I've worked with than before — who will fill out the group and add to its total sound. You certainly have the skills and experience we need but I feel that it is necessary for me to maintain my independence and integrity as a ~~musician~~ musician and want to take the risk of developing a group myself. You are one of the most important elements in the group I dream of but so are the rest of the musicians. Please understand my concerns and join us to make new music.

Emmett

July 30, 1980

Dear Capitol EM,

What you say goes within and all around me... I'll join you bu t-- when you feel the power of the General you'll regret demoting me to the ranks.

Its the music that counts and as any General knows the infantry is more important than the congress and the privates are more important than the majors;

JD the General Private First Class

Aug 2, 1980

Dear first class General,

The gump has to work out. It will make new music, create new words, a new world of sound. We'll get together for the first time at Rugg's next Sunday at 2 in the afternoon. They agreed to let us use their sound system and the place to rehearse on off hours in exchange for performing several gigs for them.

WE'RE ON THE WAY!

Emmett

August 5, 1980

Dear Gold,

Check. I'm still with you but not yet convinced of my ~~[illegible]~~ rank.

See you at ruggs

McArthur

Sept. 7, 1980

Dear EG,

The sound is loud, the Fury fine-- we're going to make it to the top!..

My songs   your songs   OUR BAND

Its worked out fine. I feel generally good

The General

Sept 8, 1980

Dear General
Yeh the album was OK but some of the songs could have used some more work. Time to go back to the studio for our next album.

Emmett

May 10, 1981

GolD,

Haven't heard the album yet but heard it on the grapevine that we're gonna be hot!..

The General

may 17, 1981

Dear General,

Some last minute adjustments had to be made on the album. Your playing is magnificent but your songs seemed inappropriate for the concept of the album. Maybe next time.

Emmett

Donna Whitman

ATTORNEY AT LAW

663 Fifth Avenue, New York, NY 10026

July 18, 1981

Lt. Carmen Radcliffe
S.F. Police Dept. Headquarters
City Hall
San Francisco, CA 95701

Dear Carmen,

Right now I'm submerged in a hunt for the whereabouts of rock musician Emmett Gold, and need to test the waters in San Francisco, where he was last reported seen. You were such a terrific help in that 1978 art fraud case. Can you help me with this one? I need an insider to help me get a look at what the police have already found.

And of course we have lots of catching up to do. . . . How's Rick? Still teaching karate? And Peter--he must be dating by now or at least trying to!

If you're interested write me soon and I'll fill you in on the situation. Or you can call me at (212)872-3511.

Dying to hear from you.

Donna

Donna Whitman

DW/lc

Donna Whitman
ATTORNEY AT LAW
663 Fifth Avenue, New York, NY 10026

July 24, 1981

Dear Howard,

This Emmett Gold is quite an interesting person. I managed to persuade a friend of mine in the San Francisco Police to let me into the hotel room where Gold was staying when he disappeared and to let me run through and photograph things he left behind. The originals of all the enclosed documents from my San Francisco trip are currently being held by the SF Police Department as part of their file on Gold.

Gold's hotel room was quite a mess, though there were no signs of any struggle. You mentioned to me that Gold liked to be private, but there must have been some kind of party going on about the time he disappeared. Inspector Radcliffe, my friend on the force, told me there were about a half dozen glasses and several bottles of champagne in the sitting room. The glasses and bottles are now out for fingerprinting. It seems that, in order to protect his reputation, the promoter of Gold's SF concert called in the police as soon as he learned that Gold was missing.

In addition to those signs of a party, the bedroom was in chaos with the sheets and covers thrown around. In fact, one maid complained about a missing sheet and told me that rock groups always take the linens. It's true, they're usually used to wrap the instruments in before putting them in the cases. A good sheet with a little silk or satin is worth a lot as a tour souvenir. I have a small collection myself from when I used to tour with Rivals.

Gold didn't leave much behind--just a suitcase, toilet items, pill bottles, plane tickets, and pages torn out from what must have been a long diary. None of the pages were current. They must have been remembrances of his life off the road that he carried when he travelled--maybe to keep himself sane. Copies of all the diary pages, pill bottle labels, and plane tickets are enclosed, as well as photos of the other items. They make me want to get to know him. Also, baggage claim tickets and a menu were found in the bedroom with scribblings on them that I can't make sense of. I've photographed them and included copies for your perusal.

Also enclosed are copies of Gold's phone messages.

By the way, on my return from SF I stopped off in Tennessee (that will unfortunately add to my expenses on the case) to interview Emmett's mother and sniff around a bit to see if any of his old friends knew where he might have run to. Enclosed is a partial transcript of that interview as well as some letters his mother let me copy.

We must get together soon. I don't feel good about this case. I'm worried for Gold.

Sincerely,

Donna

Donna Whitman

DW/lc

BREAKFAST

HOT CAKES AND WAFFLES

Buttermilk Pancakes, Dollar Pancakes
or Belgian Waffles 4.95
with Bacon, Ham or Sausages 6.45
Blueberry Pancakes or Crisp
French Toast 5.45
with Bacon, Ham or Sausages 6.95

THE ABOVE ARE SERVED WITH SWEET BUTTER, PURE VERMONT MAPLE SYRUP OR WHOLE FRUIT SYRUP

FROM THE BAKERY BASKET

Croissants 2.35 English Muffin 2.00
Danish Pastries 2.35
Cinnamon Toast 2.00
Brioches 2.35 Muffins 2.20
Selection of White, Whole Wheat, Rye,
French Bread or Raisin Toast 1.95

BEVERAGES

A Selection of Imported Teas 1.50
English Breakfast
Orange Pekoe
Earl Grey
Darjeeling
Natural Herb
Oolong
Queen Mary
Coffee 1.95
Decaffinated Coffee 1.95
Hot Chocolate with Whipped
Cream 1.85
Milk, Skim Milk 1.50

LUNCH

Available 12:00 noon to 2:30 pm
Please ask for the specials of the day.

APPETIZERS

Terrine of Vegetables with
Fresh Tomato Sauce 4.95
Jumbo Shrimp with Cocktail
or Marie-Rose Sauce 8.95
Chilled Melon with Port Wine 3.95
Terrine of Rabbit with
Compote of Nectarine 7.25
Smoked Scottish Salmon 10.50
Terrine of Foie Gras with Port Wine Aspic 19.50

SOUPS

Soup of the Day 3.50
Leek and Onion Soup Flavoured
with Vermouth 5.25
Chicken Consomme 5.50

LUNCHEON ENTREES

The Roast of the Day, served with
Salad Selection of the Day 9.75
Fresh Fish of the Day 13.75
Veal Paillard Broiled and Garnished with Brochette
of Vegetables and Bearnaise Sauce 15.25
New York Minute Sirloin Broiled
and served with Herb Butter 17.50

THE ABOVE ENTREES ARE SERVED WITH FRESH VEGETABLES AND POTATO OF THE DAY

Fresh Fruit Salad with Honey
and Yoghurt Dressing 9.50
Salade Moderne 10.75
Boston Lettuce, Vegetables and Fruit
topped with Avocado and Pacific Shrimp

For Lunch Boxes or Complete Picnic Baskets, please call Room Service the night before.

A 16% gratuity charge will be added to your bill.

DINNER

AVAILABLE 6:00 PM TO 11:00 PM
OR, ASK FOR THIS EVENINGS SPECIALTIES.
THE ENTREES LISTED BELOW ARE SERVED WITH FRESH VEGETABLES AND POTATO OF THE DAY

DINNER ENTREES

Breast of Chicken in a Pink Grapefruit and Lime Sauce 15.50
Roast Rack of Lamb and Julienne of Vegetables
in a Port Wine Sauce 22.50
Grilled Salmon with Parsley Sauce and Apple 18.00
Broiled Tenderloin of Beef with Brochette of Vegetables
and Bearnaise Sauce 21.00
Broiled New York Sirloin with Brochette of Vegetables
and Bearnaise Sauce 21.00

SALADS

Boston Salad with Walnuts and Tarragon Dressing 4.00
Romaine Lettuce with Four Seasons Dressing 3.75
Mixed Seasonal Salad, Vinaigrette 3.50

DESSERTS

Selection of Sorbets and
Ice Cream 3.25
All of our Sorbets and Ice Creams
are made with the
finest and freshest ingredients in
our Pastry Shop.
Assorted Fruit Flans 3.50
Caramel Cream 2.75
Four Seasons' Cheesecake with
Strawberry Sauce 3.50
Selection of Two French Pastries 3.75
Imported and Domestic Cheese Plate
with Fruits, Bread and
Imported Cheeses 5.25

BEVERAGES

Coffee 1.95
Decaffinated Coffee 1.95
Selection of Imported
Teas 1.50
Darjeeling
Earl Grey
Oolong
Queen Mary
Orange Pekoe
Natural Herb
Milk 1.50
Skim Milk 1.50

A 16% gratuity charge will be added to your bill.

EXHIBIT
A

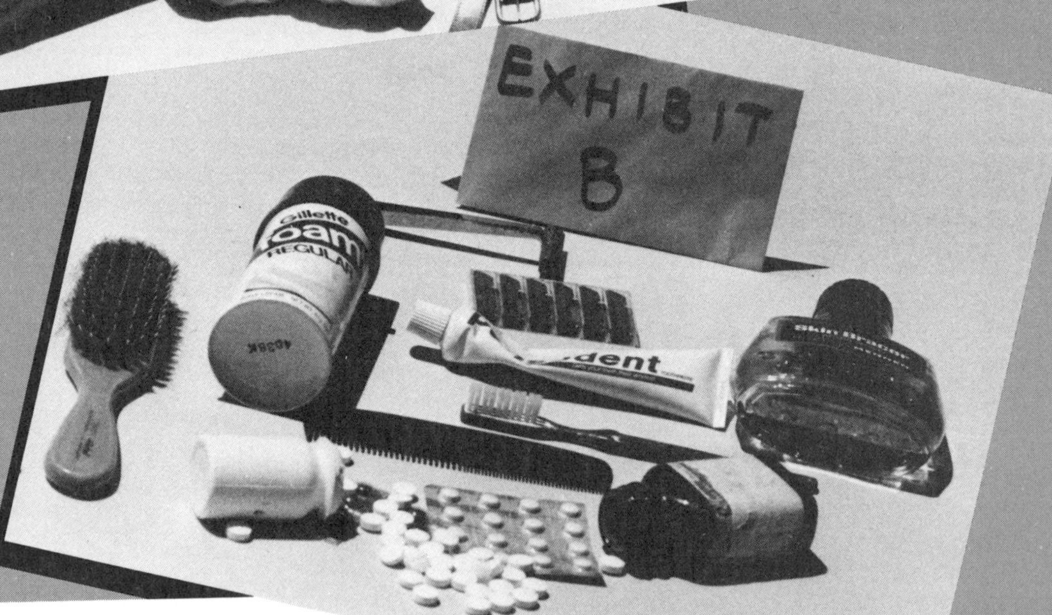
EXHIBIT
B
Gillette
Foam
REGULAR

NORTHWEST ORIENT
734-852
734-850
YOUR BAG IS
CHECKED TO
SAN FRANCISCO
05-4696
UNITED AIRLINES
SFO

NORTHWEST ORIENT
FLIGHT
DATE
call Frost
Liza
(not austin)
DESTINATION
SEAT
GATE
FLIGHT
DATE
157
7/10/81
DESTINATION
SEAT
GATE
14H
WINDOW/NO SMOKING
4
LAST NAME
PRIOR
TIME
ISSUED BY
AUTHORIZED AGENT

To Emmett Gold

Date July 8 Time 6:30 pm A.M. P.M.

WHILE YOU WERE OUT

Mr. J.D. MacArthur

of Mirage

Phone ext. 1114
Area Code Number Extension

TELEPHONED	x	PLEASE CALL	
CALLED TO SEE YOU		WILL CALL AGAIN	
WANTS TO SEE YOU		RUSH	
	RETURNED YOUR CALL		

Message Had to replace you at rehearsal. Didn't miss you at all. Watch out.

hl/St. Francis Hotel
Operator

To Emmett Gold

Date July 9 Time 7pm A.M. P.M.

WHILE YOU WERE OUT

Ms. Helen Roberts

of xxxxxxxxxxxxx

Phone xxxxxxxxxxx
Area Code Number Extension

TELEPHONED	x	PLEASE CALL	
CALLED TO SEE YOU		WILL CALL AGAIN	
WANTS TO SEE YOU		RUSH	
	RETURNED YOUR CALL		

Message Reservations confirmed 7:00 at Enricos on the 11th.

hl/St. Francis Hotel
Operator

To Emmett Gold

Date July 10 Time 10am A.M. P.M.

WHILE YOU WERE OUT

Mr. Jim Austin

of Mirage

Phone ext. 1024
Area Code Number Extension

TELEPHONED	x	PLEASE CALL	x
CALLED TO SEE YOU		WILL CALL AGAIN	
WANTS TO SEE YOU		RUSH	
	RETURNED YOUR CALL		

Message Need to have a serious talk with you regarding Liza.

js/St. Francis Hotel
Operator

To Emmett Gold

Date July 10 Time 11:30am A.M. P.M.

WHILE YOU WERE OUT

Ms. Janice Rockwell

of xxxxxxxxxxx

Phone xxxxxxxxxx
Area Code Number Extension

TELEPHONED	x	PLEASE CALL	
CALLED TO SEE YOU		WILL CALL AGAIN	x
WANTS TO SEE YOU	x	RUSH	
	RETURNED YOUR CALL		

Message You always avoid me. I'm coming up next time.

js/St. Francis Hotel
Operator

To Emmett Gold

Date July 10 Time 4pm A.M. P.M.

WHILE YOU WERE OUT

Ms. Liza Willow

of Mirage

Phone ext. 902

Area Code Number Extension

TELEPHONED	x	PLEASE CALL	
CALLED TO SEE YOU		WILL CALL AGAIN	
WANTS TO SEE YOU		RUSH	
	RETURNED YOUR CALL		

Message Had lunch with Frost about new contracts. I think I ought to talk to you.

jd St. Francis Hotel

Operator

To Emmett Gold

Date July 10 Time 5:45 pm A.M. P.M.

WHILE YOU WERE OUT

Mr. Howard Frost

of HF Artists Representative

Phone 213-567-5544

Area Code Number Extension

TELEPHONED	x	PLEASE CALL	
CALLED TO SEE YOU		WILL CALL AGAIN	
WANTS TO SEE YOU		RUSH	
	RETURNED YOUR CALL		

Message Meet you at Vanessi's for lunch 1:00 on the 13th. Call if you can't make it.

hl/St. Francis Hotel

Operator

Wright's Pharmacy

Point Arena, CA

Janet Tucker, Pharmacist

CAUTION: Federal law prohibits transfer of this drug to any person other than patient for whom prescribed.

KEEP ALL MEDICINES OUT OF CHILDREN'S REACH

DISCARD AFTER 3/85

#306854

EMMETT GOLD Dr. Prince

5/30/81imf

Take one tablet at bedtime if needed for sleep.

Quaalude-300 #100

Wright's Pharmacy

Point Arena, CA

Janet Tucker, Pharmacist

CAUTION Federal law prohibits transfer of this drug to any person other than patient for whom prescribed

KEEP ALL MEDICINES OUT OF CHILDREN'S REACH

DISCARD AFTER 6/83

#306856 Dr. Prince

EMMETT GOLD 5/30/81imf

Take one tablet three times a day as directed for weight control.

Dexadrine 5mg #100

March 4 1968

Dear diary (some day I'm going to give you a name)

Last night I awoke in my sleep. The strangest chill ran up and down my spine. It was telling me something. I needed something more in my life. There was an empty space somewhere at school. I'm never the one to be fussed over. But yes there is something I have band. Music class is the only time of the day where I am myself. I always have to have some kind of front — I don't know — maybe to prove I'm no loser. When the 5th bell rings and everyone rushes to 5th period class I can feel myself changing. Knowing that I can show my feelings during class — be the person I am at home around dad the person I love and admire the most in the whole wide world.

I'm a whole other person but one 45 minute class isn't enough of that wonderful feeling for me. I need more time in my life for the thing I do and makes me feel the best. When I listen to dad pick out some of his songs I have this thing inside of me saying that I've got to get away from the shallow school music no matter that its the best school got. But how can I fulfill all of my dreams, feelings and needs ? ?

I ~~[illegible]~~ won't say I'm friendless for it hurts me deeply making a large dent in my insides pushing out tears every time I think of it— but dad and his union friends are my only true friends who share my beliefs sorrows joys and my love of music. I'm in desperate search of a friend—just one I can talk to, share my music my thoughts. Someone who will bring out my ~~confidence~~ confidence I know I'M NO LOSER

and deep inside me is a winning
soul. So please GOD, help me
find myself through the strength and
love of a friend.

I think I'll sleep tonight.

Emmett

March 22, 1968

Dear Abraham (how's that for a distinguished diary name?)

Today ~~last w~~ the most wonderful thing happened to me. This may seem strange but the wonderful thing is that I quit the band!! Let me explain. I walked into the band room while Robert Barker, a one fine drummer (He seems to be very talented) was arguing with the music teacher. As Mr. Quebec was trying to persuade Robert not to quit Robert came up with all the nine reasons to quit. I listened intently as I foolishly eavesdropped on the two. It came to my mind that Robert was expressing all of my deepest feelings. Finally, someone who understood. He felt the same as I did—the need for feeling in music. It was as if he was reading my mind. I got ahold of Robert as he was storming out the door and shared my feelings. He suggested we work

together on our needs and hopes.
I've found and got hold of a
good thing. I just pray I can
keep hold of it.

April 1, 1968

Dear Abe,

MUTT and JEFF!! What a
success. Our leave of the school band
sure was a great loss to them but I
definitely came out ahead!! The kids
love us. We may be the first student
band but the school sure needs it.
This is fun, YEA, and more what
I call music than the school band.
I know that someday in the future
maybe not too far in the future either
one damn thing I know for sure
is that my music will make it.
Maybe not this year but soon. I
need to leave this place. There are places
I have to go to and things I need
to learn that can't be done in a
small Tennessee holler like this.
Another year or two of Mutt and Jeff—
After that Emmett sees the world.

January 20, 1970

Dear old Abraham,

Well, I'm on my way. Now my life will begin. It's not like I'm running away. I told everybody where I was off to.

I just hope that Rob understands. I don't want him to think that I'm deserting him. I know someday I'm commin' back for him. We'll play together. I'm going to Europe to expand myself, get away from the mountains. I just pray that Rob leaves for a while. I love these mountains, their people, my home but if ol Jeff wants to be more than ol Jeff he'd better get out.

When I get back I want to see Robert Barker a trained, experienced musician — he'd better put his darned talent to use!

I know mom understands and respects my decision to leave but I just worry about her. She has so much to take care of, the farm, the kids — and no man in the house. I love her and feel guilty — but at this point it seems as if there is nothing I can do here if I want to enter the music world. Jr. is getting older and he'll be the biggest help to ma. I'll be fine away from home just so long as

she keeps in touch and assures me that everyone and everything is fine back home.
I'm ON MY WAY ——
just hope I'm taking the right way!

On tour

I know I haven't written
in a long time but I feel
a need. It's Liza. Now that
I'm in New York hitting
it off pretty well with my
new band, and spending time
with Mutt again it seems
like I've got everything.
Yea— I'm happy. I just hate
to see Liza with someone
else. I knew I shouldn't have
dragged her into the band I
knew she would have changed,
started a new life and
wanted no part of me now but
I had to see her, look at the
face that I spent days and
days with only one year ago.
I've been dreaming about her
playing with our names—

LIZA AZIL AZUL the
beautiful calm sea

LIZA AL 12 is all for
me EM METT Liza I
This is too silly ——
I thought she might
remember those days when she
joined the band and maybe—
just maybe talk with me.
But now when I look at
her with love in my eyes
she just avoids me as if it
hurts to remember. I think
she still cares but is afraid
to let herself show affection
towards me.
I want to talk to her but
I'm so afraid of rejection,
which Liza introduced to me
in our early Europe days. I'll
give it time, let her realize I
still care and approach her when
the time is right. While I'm
waiting I'll just have to go on back to living
in a one sided love affair.

Emmett

Donna Whitman
ATTORNEY AT LAW
663 Fifth Avenue, New York, NY 10026

Transcript of my interview with Mrs. Gold
Mt. View Hollow, Tennessee
July 23, 1981

W: Mrs. Gold, I know that this disappearance must be hard for you, but would you mind sharing a few things about Emmett? It's for the good of finding out the whereabouts of your son.

G: I would be more than glad to help in any way.

W: Is it a surprise to you that your son has disappeared or taken an unknown trip?

G: My Emmett was a child always to be looked over. He was very strong and capable of taking care of himself but he had these sudden urges to go somewhere odd or do something different. You may call him a bit restless. I knew him very well and I could tell that Emmett was always sure of what he was doing and he had his own important reasons.

Emmett may like to leave at odd times but this time I'm worried. Not one time has he left without informing his late father Kenneth, me, or his wonderful companion Robert. He may have told us one minute before he left but he never failed to make sure we all knew that he wasn't deserting his family or friends or life for that matter.

W: How was Emmett's relationship with his father Kenneth?

G: Kenneth was a hard-working man, a wonderful one too. Emmett saw no bad in his pa. He loved him more than anyone. They really were quite a pair. I still get tears in my eyes when I see pictures of the two of them together.

W: How old was Emmett when Kenneth died?

G: Emmett was sixteen and living with his aunt. Emmett was sent for to come take care of me and his brothers. Emmett didn't take his father's death in a hard way. I remember the day I had a long talk with him on the tallest hill on our holler. He would say, "Ma, I know this is hard for you but Pa was a strong man, has accomplished a proud life of hard work and good love. He has made people think about life and has taught me all I know. If there was anything else Pa wanted to show or prove I think he would have pulled through. He led a brave life and I think he wanted it ended as it was. If there is anything he left undone I promise I will carry it out. I owe it to him." And when my Emmett held his arms around me we cried, because of how special his life was to us and the world.

One thing that Kenneth did leave behind was his guitar. That was his pride and glory. He left it to Emmett and enclosed in the guitar case was a beautiful song he wrote. I guess he wanted Emmett to figure it out and play it himself. Miss Whitman, I don't think that Emmett would ever dream of disappointing his people back home.

W: I know that there are bad times back in Mountain View Hollow. Has Emmett supported you at all since his introduction with stardom?

G: Emmett has always helped us out. Visits when possible. Writes frequently, and, yes, he does send us money.... I'm worried. No check, letter, call, or trace has come from him since he wrote saying he was ready to leave for his San Francisco tour. I know he would have told me if he was to go elsewhere.

W: Thank you Mrs. Gold. You really helped. I hope this little talk didn't upset you more. I'm glad you care so much. I'll fill you in on all the details as they come.

transcribed by lc

Oct 7, 1969

Mom,

I'm ready to come home and take care of you all. I just can't believe that dad had to go so soon. His spirit was so strong that he will always be with me guiding me assuring me as I grow. My bags are packed. I already bid my friends goodbye. Thanks for the guitar. I know I'll use it but I don't feel much like singing now. I'm waiting.

Love,

Emmett

Nov 20, 1970

Mom,

I promised to keep in touch and that's just what I'm doing. Each day I learn a new thing and I know Paris is doing good for me. I know it must be hard for you back home but this is a very important time in my life and I can't stop now. I've got great teachers and meet people who are now very special to me. I met a wonderful intelligent lady. She is very important to me and I'd like you to meet her some day. I hope you're getting along OK back home. Send Jr., Petey, and Clint my love.

I miss you,

Emmett

New Paris Sound: Fusion Jazz

Barney Robertson has been a central figure on the Paris jazz scene since he settled here in 1951. As a performer, teacher, and father figure to many young artists he has gained the reputation of being a musician's musician. He is a regular at Le Club Feu where he often sits in with guest performers as well as playing piano, sax, and even acoustic guitar with his own trio. As Ornette Coleman said of him, "Barney's the glue, the cement, the spirit of any group he plays in. He's always pushing us—not to show he's better—but to teach us how good we can be. There's no slacking off when Barney's around."

We thought we'd ask Robertson for his assessment of the current jazz scene in Paris.

"These last two years have seen major changes on the jazz scene. When I first came here most of us had been trained in the clubs. I did some time in the service and saw Paris at the end of World War II but New York was where I had to be. Jazz, serious jazz, was alive on Broadway and 7th Avenue in the late forties. Old forms were broken, young musicians were coming in from all over the country with skills and big band experience. There was an air of freedom and celebration, of breaking old forms, escaping boring big bands, and going beyond Dixie. Then the fifties hit—my politics and those of the Senator from Wisconsin weren't exactly the same, so I politely left for Paris—not just me but lots of us left because of politics and Jim Crow. We made our music here where we were more welcome, where jazz was music of dignity—not back-alley stuff."

Robertson paced as he talked, fingering the instruments that almost buried the furniture in his small Latin Quarter apartment. He has one of the finest collections of antique instruments in Paris and some of his students claim he can play them all.

"There's a whole new breed of musicians invading Paris these days, youngsters with different skills and backgrounds than my generation—'fusion musicians' I call them. They come from all over—Holland, Sweden, Italy, England. They know jazz, they have some training and experience, but they have no cultural background for jazz. They feel for it but are searching for their own music. Jazz calls to them because it is possible to be complex and free; they know how to play notes and don't only want to play notes.

"There's a new exodus from the States too—black and white musicians who aren't afraid to play any kind of music, who are searching for new forms."

The phone rang and Robertson excused himself. It was a long-distance call from a studio in Amsterdam that wanted him for a recording session.

When the conversation was over he explained that he spent time as a music doctor. He travels a lot to recording studios to dub piano or sax parts to help rescue records the producers feel are flat and lifeless.

Robertson returned to the contemporary jazz scene in Paris:

"The fusion musicians are good and they're going to be excellent if pop music and money doesn't provide too much of a temptation for them. There are two youngsters in particular to watch for. Hans Halberstad is a young Dutch trumpet player. I think people listen to more serious jazz in Holland then anywhere else in the world with the exception of Tokyo."

Robertson looked troubled and continued after pacing for awhile.

"I wish it were New York and not Japan. Anyway, Hans has a feel for Miles Davis, a tune that is classical and a wildness that when it gets reined in and controlled will cut the fine line between traditional classical music and serious jazz. You can hear him at the Club 76 several days a week and it's worth staying to the last set when he reaches out and starts exploring his own musical ideas.

"And there's Emmett Gold, a complex and immature musician form. He came here a year ago loving music and knowing nothing about it. I met him one night at Le Club Feu. A friend of his from Amsterdam took him to hear my trio play.

"Gold is a slow learner; he listens a lot before he tries anything himself. I noticed him in the audience every night for a month and tried to persuade him to sit in with us on our last set Tuesday nights—just about nobody's in the club then and it's a good time to let youngsters sit in with us tired old musicians. He refused to join us until about a month of listening. Then one Tuesday he sat in, playing everything he heard. He must have learned half my riffs and practiced for hours—until he was ready to come out. Only he added something I never heard before, a fiddle down-tuning on his guitar that added a touch of folk and country music. I never cared for that tradition but it's a driving force in his music. He's so good he might become popular too soon and lose the serious part of himself.

"You can hear him at Le Club Feu Tuesdays and on weekends where he plays second guitar in the warm-up band."

As a final note, Robertson said that the best buy in jazz in Paris today was not at the clubs but at Filbert's rehearsal studios. The price of admission, he said, was a serious concern for the future of jazz.

July 21, 1981

Dear Ms. Whitman,

I feel very awkward writing to you like this, but I have heard that you are trying to discover what happened to Emmett Gold. You're probably aware that I am the saxophonist in Mirage. You may not know, however, that Emmett and I were very close friends and at one time years ago in Paris lovers. It is important for you to understand that Emmett is not just another rock musician. His music is currently in a rock stage, but he has a restless brilliant mind and is constantly growing and experimenting. It is awkward for me to be in the band, and I don't love Emmett in the same way I used to, but I cannot stay away from his music. He has been a driving creative force for many musicians, and no matter what our personal relationship you must understand that I care for his growth and his career. Jim Austin does too despite the fact that Jim and I live together and care for each other in a way Emmett could never understand. We have both heard rumors about Emmett leaving the band because of us, and I want to assure you that it could not be true. Emmett, Jim and I have worked out an arrangement which is purely professional and which utilizes each of our special skills in the service of our music. Personal relationships do not get in the way of our creativity.

There is friction in the band, but I assure you it does not come from us. I do not like to tell tales, but I urge you to talk with Rob Bangor if you want to know the truth about this miserable tour or talk with Jim and me. We are available at your convenience.

By the way I'm enclosing letters Emmett sent to me and a note that I found backstage in an open guitar case. They might interest you. This exit in San Fransisco is just not like Emmett. I'm worried.

Liza Willow

Liza,

June 1, 1970

Last night was wonderful! My first week in Amsterdam and already hearing and meeting so many great ~~musicians~~ musicians (one being you). But I bet we could have an even more wonderful night alone. I'd like to get to know you better. You stand out from all those other beautiful saxes. Try and get back to me. 251-0101. I wanna see you soon.

Emmett

Jan. 20, 1980

TO OLD FRIEND LIZA
432 A West End Ave.
NY 10027

Dear Liza,
Long time, no see! What have you
been up to? Me? A lot! Actually
That's why I'm writing. After you
left Europe I still stayed on a while.
I learned to be a fine musician and
felt it was time to be moving on. New
York was my goal. That's where I am
now. I wanna get together a new band.
I know you told me to back off, but I
want it to have quality. That's why
I'm writing to Liza Willow, wonderful
talented person. I know ~~that~~ this will
take a lot of your time and change your
life, as it is mine, but I need you now.
Good pay, recognition and maybe even some
good times together are all guaranteed. Please
reply quickly. I plan on getting started
any day now.

Sincerely,
Emmett

(My address: 324 W Dallas, NY 10005)

July 9, 1981

Liza,

I'm going through another change. Fame isn't what I want. I already have enough money to help the family back home and to spend time growing as a musician. The band isn't helping any. I need to get out and grow and learn more about music and myself. I want to make a point with my music. I'm not here to make fans scream and cheer.

What next? Mirage days are over. I'm not sure what follows. Maybe someday soon we could get together and talk.

Emmett

July 20, 1981

Dear Liza,

How about dinner tonight? Now I don't have to worry about you possibly having other plans. See, what did I tell you!?! When Emmett's gone, we're like a couple made in heaven.

I would have left if this hadn't happened. I couldn't stand to be around when he gave you those little smiles and looks, always with stars in his eyes. Now I have you all to myself. And I'd like to take you out tonight to the restaurant of your choice. Any place any price.

I know you cared about Emmett but it's done now and the best thing for you to do would be to forget about it and start all over with me. Hopefully seeya tonight,

Your only love,

Jim

EM,

The General is grateful for the golden key
to heaven. It would have been hard nights o
sidewalk without a crash pad.

like I said before, I won't let a
where it is or what it's for, just

Stars

July 16, 1981

Dear Donna,

Heard that you are trying to chase down the whereabouts of my dear friend/colleague Emmett Gold. I don't know if I'll be any help to you but I'd like to find him in any way possible. You probably know that Gold had a very messed up childhood. With his father dead and his mother always in need of help you never know where he could have gone to. Last I saw him was at the hotel in San Francisco where the band was being put up. I don't know what was bugging him--it must have been the road. Even my stories didn't liven him up. I don't think that Mirage can survive without him.

Maybe you heard about that crazy groupie that followed us around on tour. Emmett may just be trying to get away from fans and that sort of people. Groupies can drive xxx someone crazy. They think you belong to them just because they buy your records and see your shows.

If you need any help get ahold of me. I've got alot of connections in the music underworld. You can leave a message for me with Howard Frost.

J.D. McArthur

HOWARD FROST
Artists' Representative

4071 Madrone Boulevard
Los Angeles, California 89701

July 23, 1981

Dear Donna,

Here is our Ms. Little Red on the front page of the National Inquisitor. Do you think you could trace her down and find out whether she actually knows an ything about Gold? I can't believe he would waste his time with anyone like her but you can never tell what happens on the road.

Sincerely,

Howard

Howard Frost

GROUPIE TELLS ALL

"He was gonna take me with him! After I followed him through all the states, excited by his every move, I could tell that he finally fell for me."

As "Little Red" sits all sprawled out on the floor of her exotically decorated roadie van we catch a few words about the very blurry disappearance of rock star Emmett Gold.

"I knew Emmett inside out. He was waiting . . ." Red pauses as if not knowing what to say next. "He loved me . . . I knew he was trying to find me . . . take me back to New York with him . . ."

Ms. Red paused to take a drag on what looked like a hand-rolled cigarette.

Little Red almost makes five feet though she carries enough weight for a six footer. She was born in Schenectady, New York and as she puts it "almost graduated Schenectady High."

We talked to Red about her love affair with Rock and Roll. She said she goes back a ways. "It began with Otis Redding and Mary Wells. I used to go to all the clubs in Schenectady, to pretend I was twenty when I was fourteen. It's crazy but I fell in love with this drummer. He was married but I didn't care. It took three months for me to date him. When he finally asked me out it turned out to be boring."

Red sighed and mentioned all the other musicians she had known. Then she turned serious:

"Emmett was different. He wasn't just a musician on the run. He knew about everything, was serious about life and politics, had dreams about music. The first time I heard him talk, not play music, but talk, in a bar on 7th Avenue after an amateur night at Julie's, I fell in love. He didn't notice me then but after awhile he had to recognize my face. There were nights when I was the only one in his audience—oh, maybe there were a few other people but I was always there."

Little Red brushed a tear from her eye and sighed. Then she took out her Emmett Gold scrapbook and leafed through clippings and ads that seemed to cover all the work of Gold and the Mirages from the time they were organized. She paused to reminisce about the last time she'd seen him, at the Portland concert.

"I entered the show late at the very end . . . front row . . . my Emmett didn't see me waiting in my seat hours before the show as usual. I knew when he didn't see me there he went and offed himself. He couldn't face my absence!"

As we talk to Red she sobs as if the world is at end. We're suspicious of Red. Did she even know Emmett personally? The only reply we get when we ask such questions is a desperate, "Did I know him?! He was a part of me!"

Was Emmett in love? Is this groupie a wishful dreamer? Will we ever find out?

NATIONAL INQUISITOR

July 22, 1981

I M P O R T A N T !

July 26, 1981   8:30 AM

Donna --

Carmen Radcliffe called from SFPD with urgent news. Call her immediately.

Lori

I M P O R T A N T !

western union

Telegram

CARMEN, THE NEWS WAS DEPRESSING. LEAVING FOR SF FLIGHT #276 PANAM ARRIVING 5:45PM. MEET ME. WOULD APPRECIATE YOU TAKE TIME TO 1) GET KEY ROOM 18 STREET, LET LANDLORD KNOW I'LL BE INVESTIGATING. 2) MAKE LIST OF WHAT'S FOUND IN ROOM, CURRENTLY HELD BY SFPD. PHOTOS TOO. 3) ARRANGE TIME TO LOOK AT BODY.

NEWS HASN'T HIT NEW YORK YET. WOULD APPRECIATE HOLDING BACK PUBLICITY LONG AS POSSIBLE.

DONNA

ATTORNEY AT LAW 663 FIFTH AVENUE NEW YORK NY 10026

W.U. 1201-SF (R5-69)

July 26, 1981

Donna,

I couldn't make it to the airport because the case I'm currently working on brings me to North Beach tonight. I gave the material to Sergeant Reynolds, a good friend of mine. He has all my written information, some photos, plus the key you requested.

He'll fill you in on the details and drive you to the apartment as soon as he's off shift.

I will be able to meet you tomorrow over lunch and afterwards we will be able to see Gold.

Carmen
SFPD

The San Francisco Voice, July 27, 1981

Gold Discovered!

Many people—fans, friends, and family—have been clinging tightly to the word "disappearance," as in the "disappearance of Emmett Gold," hoping that the word would not change to "death." Last night those hopes were shattered when Gold was found dead in a small apartment on the border of the Mission District. The apartment was not extravagant, but, for reasons unknown to even his closest friends, Gold chose it as his roof for his short stay in San Francisco. Gold, who had registered at the Knob Hill Inn for his San Francisco visit, had apparently kept the whereabouts of the Mission Hill apartment a close secret.

Authorities attribute the death to a possible drug overdose. However, the only drug found on the scene was a half-smoked marijuana cigarette.

Suicide and foul play have not been ruled out. The San Francisco Police Department has mounted a mammoth investigation and expects to release results soon.

July 27, 1981

TO: Donna Whitman
Hotel Fairmont

FROM: Carmen Radcliffe
SFPD

Following is a list of properties found at 475 West 18 Street, Room 4G:

guitar case -- guitar, song lyrics found in case (see attached)
airplane ticket (one way to Knoxville, Tennessee)
small duffel bag with miscellaneous underwear
leather jacket with contents:
A) letter from Mrs. Kenneth Gold (see attached)
B) song scribbled on napkin
C) notes from Liza Willow
D) cigarette (suspected marijuana, currently at lab)

We've also investigated the prescription labels from bottles found in the hotel room. It seems strange that Gold carried dexadrine since he was so thin. Quaaludes and dexadrine make a deadly combination. I cannot understand why Gold had them together unless he intended suicide.

That's all so far. Keep me informed. Call if you need help.

Carmen

Oct 1, 1969

Dearest Emmett,

As you know conditions are terribly bad back home. I miss you. It's so quiet back here in ol' Mountain View without your constant humming or making music with something or another. Now that dads gone it's even quieter.

Remember all those meetings you would go to with dad? I can still see you... running after Kenneth with his guitar tightly tucked under your arm! You did have a good time together didn't you?

I guess all that mine work, singing, picketing and all his other obligations became too much for a man of his age. He was a busy man. Yes, he was. I'm coming down to get you and pick you up for the funeral back home.

Let's try and make the best of it.

Love ya,

Mom ♡

XXX OOO

P.S. Dad wanted you to have his guitar and I'm holding it for you.

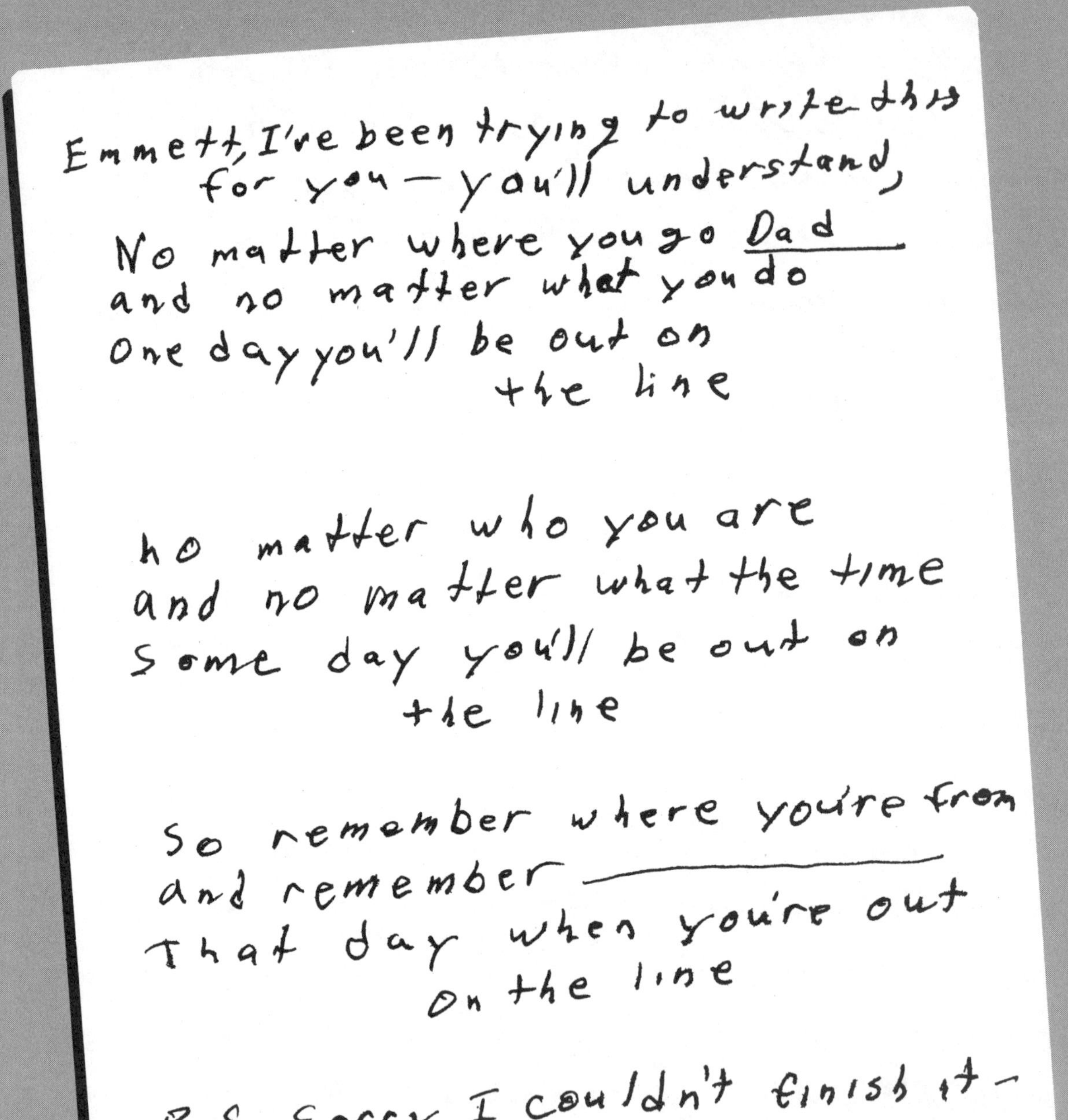

Emmett, I've been trying to write this
for you — you'll understand,

No matter where you go <u>Dad</u>
and no matter what you do
One day you'll be out on
the line

no matter who you are
and no matter what the time
Some day you'll be out on
the line

So remember where you're from
and remember ____________
That day when you're out
on the line

P. S. Sorry I couldn't finish it —
maybe you'll do it for me

When Night Turns to Morning

The music fading, the sun rising
I remember the mountains at home
and see the towers here —
Notre Dame, our double lady — whose lady?
A lady, a lazy walk home
Dragging a sax and what's left
of an old guitar
Is the hurt because of the wonders here
or the loss of the little places I
won't go to, can't go to, need
to go to again?
There is too much music in the world
For a guitar or a simple song.

Paris '71

DEAR M.......

WE'RE GONNA BE GOLD

FROST TOLD ME TO WRITE, A COLD NAME THAT MAN HAS, BUT WE'RE HOT!-GOLD AND MCARTHUR- THE CHIEFS OF STAFF OF ROCKING AND SHOUTING. HEARD YOU THE OTHER NIGHT AT JULIE'S— YOU'RE GOOD, BOY, ALMOST AS GOOD AS THE GENERAL. WE CAN BLEND AND MEND AND WEAVE TOGETHER. I'LL JOIN YOU, YOU JOIN ME, WE GOT THE WAY TO SAVE THE DAY FOR ROCK AND ROLL TODAY. I DONT JUST PLAY WITH ANYONE YOU KNOW, BUT WELL BE FINE TOGETHER— JUST ADD A LITTLE SPICE AND WELL BE NICE.

SEE YOU AT HOWIES OFFICE WED. AT 2:00

YOUR MUSICAL COMPANION, MCARTHUR LANDED NOT SOON NOT LATE, BUT ON TIME!

THE GENERAL

July 16, 1971

Dearest Emmett,

I will always love playing with you, but I just can't keep up with the pace of your life and your restlessness. It's time for me to settle into my music more, to play for myself. In some ways I'll always love you, but now you scare me and take me away from myself.

Maybe... just maybe... we can continue to play together, to be friends... but I can't let my work disappear. I know your sorrow and your anger. And yes, even though you don't like me to say it, you're a genius, but you're not right for me.

I'm off to Germany for some studio recording, don't know when I'll be back. Don't try to reach me.

Liza

Jan. 27, 1980

Dear Emmett,

I'm proud for you! I wasn't quite sure you'd make it through. Your future sounds pleasing and so does mine. I accept your offer. I just have something that I want you to know. When I said that it was over with us, I meant it. That still goes. I only take your offer under certain conditions, remember. Things between us must stay strictly musical. I am presently seeing Jim Austin. He means a lot to me, is a great musician, and I could not bear to leave him. When I join the band he joins too. If you decide you don't like him and he leaves I leave too. Otherwise,

It's a deal,

Liza

432 A West End Ave

New York, N.Y. 10027

July 10, 1981

Dear Emmett,

Thinking back on these past few years I can't quite recall where you stood in my life: friend, ex-lover, music associate. Maybe none of these either. I haven't been in my right mind for quite a while.

Recently I've been able to see stress in you; and feel it in me. Then I look back on those days we shared in Europe. I felt free. Saying what I thought, doing as I pleased was easier in those days. My memories linger but we seem to drift apart.

I have been foolish. Don't you see we need each other? Please don't feel I rejected you. I thought Austin was what I needed, apparently not. I need you Emmett. I love you. Sorry about my wildness. I'm straightening up. I want to see you tonight, alone.

Yours,

Liza

Donna Whitman
ATTORNEY AT LAW
663 Fifth Avenue, New York, NY 10026

July 25, 1981

Dear Carmen,

I finally had a chance to interview Jim Austin, but only by phone. Austin seemed cold and remote, and the last words he said in the interview were these: "His disappearance is too bad, but it's no big tragedy to me. It takes him off of my woman. I was waiting for him to get off of her case."

Have you dug up any new information on Austin or on any of the other band members?

Donna

Donna Whitman

DW/lc

Donna Whitman
ATTORNEY AT LAW
663 Fifth Avenue, New York, NY 10026

July 31, 1981

Dear Carmen,

Thank you for sending the coroner's report on the death of Emmett Gold. I was not surprised to discover that he died of a combination of quaaludes, dexadrine, and liquor. But I disagree with the preliminary conclusion of accident or suicide. What especially surprised me was the laboratory finding that the paper of the marijuana cigarette found in the apartment where the body was discovered was soaked with the highly poisonous STP. Somebody clearly wanted Gold dead or at least disfunctional. It is unlikely that Gold would have smoked the joint if he had known what was in the paper.

There are other things that imply that the death was not accidental and that Gold was not suicidal. The ticket to Knoxville found with the body indicated that Gold intended to see his mother and did have some plans for the future. The letter from Willow indicated that Gold's personal life wasn't all that grim. Also, the interviews from the papers indicated that Gold had many musical dreams for his future. Now why would Gold want to put an end to such a promising life?

There are several people who could have reasons to kill Gold and I have considered them one by one and tried to make sense out of the clues we have gathered.

First, there is Jim Austin, the pianist and arranger in the band. His comments to me about Gold's disappearance indicated very little sorrow and showed him to be jealous and protective of his relationship with Liza Willow. Also, there was a phone number for Liza Willow on one of the airplane claim checks found in Gold's hotel room. I was puzzled by the fact that two of the claim checks were for Northwest Orient Airlines and one for United. Willow's phone number was on the United claim check. On researching the matter I discovered that Gold did not fly United, but that other band members did. This leads me to believe that someone either inadvertantly left the ticket in Gold's room or planted it there to point suspicion at Jim Austin.

The second suspect is Gold's old friend Rob Bangor. However, no clues point toward him and he has been very helpful to me during the investigation. He is in great shock and very depressed and has not been seen in public since the disappearance. But he may be trying to hide something.

The third suspect is Gold's agent, Howard Frost, the man who hired me to investigate the case in the first place. I have been corresponding with him throughout the case and developed mixed feelings about him. Frost and Gold were in the process of negotiating a new long-term contract for pop music at a time when Gold was interested in playing a far more serious type of music. As his agent Frost had no hold on Gold, because the original contract gave Gold the the option of terminating at any time. Frost stood to lose a lot of money if Gold left and created modern music on his own. With Gold dead, Frost could reissue all the Emmett Gold records and make money on them as nostalgia items. I hope I'm not being too hard on Frost but the telephone messages found in Gold's hotel room indicate that Frost had lunch with Liza Willow in San Francisco the day Gold disappeared, but also have him calling Gold to set up a luncheon appointment from Los Angeles (the 213 area code on his message shows that). Just where <u>was</u> Frost the day Gold disappeared?

The fourth suspect, J. D. McArthur, is a bit of a puzzle. Emmett Gold personally chose all of the band members with the exception of him. Howard Frost brought McArthur into the band probably because he needed someone with experience in the rock world. The two had worked together before. McArthur wasn't upset by Gold's disappearance and in one of the phone notes made it clear that he felt confident that he could replace Gold. A lot of bands go on and continue to be successes even though a lead performer dies or leaves. In McArthur's eyes, Mirage under his own direction could easily be as successful as Mirage under Gold.

As for the fifth suspect, "Ms. Little Red," whose real name turns out to be Janice Rockwell, it is possible that she supplied the STP-soaked marijuana cigarette. As your department found out, she is a well-known dealer to musicians. However it is not clear that Gold ever really saw her, and certainly she made a bigger deal of their so-called relationship than he ever did. However, it <u>is</u> possible that she did deliver some drugs to Gold and they partied until he died. Groupies have their ways.

Finally, the sixth suspect, Liza Willow. She seems to be such a sensitive, caring person that I simply can't bring myself to think that she's capable of murder. What I don't understand is how she got caught up in the rock world in the first place. It must have had something to do with her love of Gold and with the power of his music. Her letters cause me no suspicions, and her desire to talk with Gold the day he disappeared, after meeting with Frost, seems to have been natural and honest. But I can't eliminate her yet, because I have been fooled by innocent-seeming people before.

These are my thoughts so far. In the next week I will look more deeply into all aspects of the case and hope to come up with specific conclusions. I'll send you a copy of my final investigative report.

Sincerely,

Donna

Donna Whitman

DW/lc

Before you read Donna Whitman's final investigative report, think about the evidence and decide for yourself what happened to Emmett Gold. Write your own investigative report here:

Investigator ______________________________

Case ______________________________

Conclusions ______________________________

Investigator ______________________________

Case ______________________________

Conclusions ______________________________

Final Investigative Report

Donna Whitman
ATTORNEY AT LAW
663 Fifth Avenue, New York, NY 10026

FINAL INVESTIGATIVE REPORT
Emmett Gold case

August 2, 1981

Dear Carmen,

I'm relieved to report that my investigation of Emmett Gold's disappearance is at an end. Although I've found small reasons to suspect many people, the overwhelming evidence points in one direction--to J.D. McArthur. Someone was obviously driving Gold crazy, and the letters Frost sent me indicated that Gold's position in the band seemed threatened by McArthur from the start. In addition, McArthur was the only musician Gold did not personally bring into the band.

As you know, McArthur calls himself the "General" and wears military clothes on stage. The correspondence between Gold and McArthur showed that McArthur was desperate for higher and higher positions and wanted to become the "General" of the group. Also, I noticed on the plane ticket found in Gold's hotel room a bit of warfare between a tank and several airplanes--scenes that somehow made me think of McArthur.

There are other indications of extreme jealousy between McArthur and Gold. Gold eliminated McArthur's songs from the Lightning Strikes album, and McArthur on his resume refers to the band as "Mirage" and never as "Emmett Gold/Mirage."

There is another clue that has been bothering me. Gold scribbled "MANMAD" on a menu in his hotel room. At first I thought it referred to Jim Austin, who was indeed very mad at what was happening between Liza Willow and Emmett. But that wore off as I began to play with the letters as I imagined Gold would in his song lyrics and titles. They seemed more like a puzzle to me than a direct message. I know this may sound crazy, but "MANMAD" backwards is "DAMNAM" which could be interpreted as "damn Vietnam." McArthur is a Vietnam veteran and lets everyone know it. I see this as Gold's way of showing his own fear of and anger at McArthur.

Another clue was sent to me by Liza Willow in the form of a note from McArthur to Gold which mentioned a key to a crash pad. We know Gold checked into the hotel on July 10. We also know that a sheet was missing from the hotel room and that Gold was found dead in an apartment. This series of clues leads me to the conclusion that Emmett had been killed in the hotel, wrapped in the missing sheet, and taken to the apartment. The only evidence of someone other than Gold having possession of a key to the apartment rented by Gold is that note found in a guitar case by Liza Willow.

In the note McArthur sent me offering help he seemed to know information about Emmett's life that was contained in

Emmett's diaries found in the hotel room and in letters from his family found in the apartment. I conclude that McArthur was in both places the night of the murder.

In addition, McArthur offered me in a letter his access to the music underworld to help with this investigation. This leads me to suspect that McArthur has many ways of obtaining the illegal drugs which were found in Gold's bloodstream as well as forged prescription labels.

McArthur also told me that he could be located at Frost's phone number, the clue that first led me to suspect Frost. Given that Gold's body had to be transported from the hotel to the apartment on the night of July 10, I conclude that Frost and McArthur were working together.

Both Frost and McArthur stood to gain from Gold's death. McArthur could have taken over the lead position in the band and have his own songs recorded under the name of Mirage. Frost's position is slightly more complicated. The last note Gold sent to Liza indicated that he was changing musical direction and was ready to terminate his contract with Frost. According to the terms of the contract, Frost would then lose all claims on Gold's income. With Gold dead, the terms of the contract would last forever. In addition, Gold would be valuable to Frost as a nostalgia item and all re-releases of his work would profit Frost. There is a lot of money at stake here.

I believe there is enough evidence available for you to issue warrants against Howard Frost and J. D. McArthur for the murder of Emmett Gold.

I am sending copies of all of my investigative reports (including this one) as well as all the Gold material in my possession to the San Francisco Police Department.

Congratulations to both of us. As for the "General" and Frost, let's hope they're playing "Jailhouse Rock" for a long time to come.

Best,

Donna

Donna Whitman

DW/lc

October 1, 1982

MUSIC NOTES

GOLD REVIVAL

There has been a recent revival of the music of the late Emmett Gold. A four-album set has been released that shows us many new aspects of Gold's work. The set was produced by former Mirage band members Rob Bangor and Liza Willow. Unfortunately, Gold's former agent Howard Frost and former band member J. D. McArthur will not be able to profit from the release as they are currently serving terms at Vacaville Prison for the murder of Gold. All benefits from the album will be shared with Mrs. Kenneth Gold of Mt. View Hollow, Tennessee, the musician's mother.

Emmett Gold